READY
& Relentless

READY
& Relentless

The Marriage Book for Single Christian Women

TANESHA SHARP

BOOK TANESHA SHARP FOR YOUR NEXT
CONFERENCE, WORKSHOP, OR SEMINAR.
SEND YOUR REQUEST TO
IAMTANESHASHARP@GMAIL.COM.

Ready and Relentless
The Marriage Book for Single Christian Women
Welcome to your journey from singleness to a loving marriage.

Contents

Part 1: Ready

Part 2: Relentless

Dedication

I dedicate this book to my amazing husband Raymond and my three beautiful children Braylen, Brielle, and Bennett. This is my testimony of God's faithfulness. God will give you the desires of your heart.

I also dedicate this book to my parents Ransom and Mary Ware. They have been happily married for 38 years.

Introduction

God asked me what I would say if I could give myself premarital advice. Intrigued, I took some time to consider the insight I would provide. After giving me time for thoughtful and honest reflection, God told me to share the advice. This book will guide you through a very challenging and important process of preparing for marriage. Proper preparation for marriage will help you overcome the challenges Satan sends to disrupt the love, peace, and unity with your spouse. It is vital that you incorporate these principles into your daily life prior to marriage.

Many women have been single and saved for a long time. My goal is to give single women insight into the challenges marriages face and how to prepare themselves to become successful wives. In short, this book is for single Christian women who desire to get married and don't mind doing things God's way.

PART 1

Ready

CHAPTER 1

Hot and Ready

What's the missing ingredient?

If you bake an apple pie and leave out the apples, you will realize that something is missing: the main ingredient. Typically, our nature is to do things as quickly as possible because we are ready to move on to the next thing. Consequently, the main ingredient, which is most important, will cause us to do the most work. If it's possible to find a replacement, suitable or not, we use it instead of the correct ingredients. If we could all be honest, we don't want to do any extra work. It's in our nature to go with the flow and do as little as possible, while expecting the best possible outcome. If we are truly honest with ourselves, we do everything but the main thing, which will actually change everything. The "everything" is a perfect outcome in our lives, whether it be professionally, socially, romantically, or spiritually. In short, at the root of most individuals' lack of fulfillment is an unwillingness to do things the correct way. We need to slow down to make sure the ingredients for a great outcome are fully fleshed out, matured, and perfected before consumption. There is a reason some women are depressed, lonely, and never fulfilled in their singleness. There are probably one or two things missing. If you keep reading, you will discover your missing ingredient.

Before I got married, I felt lonely and in a constant state of discontent. Being single, in my mind, was like wearing a scarlet letter "S" that precluded me from being in any type of relationship. I felt overlooked, unwanted, undesirable, and invisible at times. I knew life was so much better for my married friends, or so I thought. What I didn't know is that you can be married and still feel lonely and unsatisfied.

I can remember the times when loneliness overwhelmed me and depression surrounded me. It seemed as if everyone around me was getting married or in a happy relationship. I constantly felt tormented by the devil. I could hear deflating discouragement enter my mind. I heard the unwelcome voices saying,

"You will never get married."

"You will never find anyone good-looking in the church."

"Settle and just accept whoever wants to marry you."

"Men don't want to get married."

"You don't have to get married."

"You can have a child with a close friend and raise the baby on your own."

"You will be too old to have kids."

"When you finally get in a relationship, it will be about five years before he proposes, and another five to eight years before you actually get married."

"You will never find the right one."

"There is no one out there for you."

It was so tempting to buy into all of these tormenting declarations. I wanted to believe the contrary, but the evidence in front of me looked more like what the enemy wanted me to receive. This is why faith is important. We must use our faith in times of temptation. Not just physical temptation, but also in times when we're tempted to receive the enemy's desires versus the desires of God. Women of God must not compromise in any area. If you compromise before marriage, you will find yourself compromising with the enemy in your marriage as well. Prior to marriage, you must receiving only God's will and purpose for your life. This will help you strengthen and undergird your husband's vision and goals without interjecting negativity unnecessarily.

I used to hold the opinion that being in a relationship equaled completion. I wanted to be desired and chased by a man. Contrarily, I would find myself being the one chasing after him, while attempting to not lose him. I always thought having a man would satisfy me. God showed me I was wrong, and that He was the only one who could satisfy me. God truly gave me this revelation right before my husband and I began to seriously date each other. Once God detoxed me from focusing on men, I was free to focus on Him and His word. I had such a desire to fast and pray. At that time in my life, I began to experience true satisfaction. I believe it only came through my hunger for God. I wanted Him more than anything. I had never been in this place with God. Before this experience, I would have doubted the possibility of God actually filling those voids in my life. Even today, after 13-plus years of marriage, I understand that my husband could never fill every void and keep me happy; only God can do that! God uses my husband at times, but he is not the only source of satisfaction and fulfillment in my life. The Bible talks about being thirsty for God (see Psalm 42:1-2). It also talks about being hungry and thirsty for righteousness and that you will be fulfilled/satisfied (see Matthew 5:6). When the Bible talks about righteousness, it means the right way of doing things according to God's word. So until we have a hunger and thirst for God and righteousness, we will never be satisfied. If you receive this revelation, it will not only bless you while you're single but also when you're married! It will help those who feel depressed and tormented by the devil.

When you're unfulfilled, you give the devil an open door to harass you. The devil's goal is to pull you further away from God and His word. The devil doesn't want you satisfied; he wants to keep you in a cycle of chasing after fulfillment and happiness. The devil wants you to believe every lie he has told you, and never be the woman/wife who is found by her husband. Your husband is going to God in prayer to find you, and God doesn't have all of you to give to him. Understand that you must be in a position to be located. If your husband is going to God in prayer about find you, but you are not connected to God in the same manner, he will not be able to find you.

We all can feel when something is off and unbalanced. We can tell when something is missing. When we haven't allowed God to make us whole, we are all unbalanced. In all of our pursuits in life and relationships, we cannot be complete without Him. No one wants to be in a relationship with an incomplete person. If you were served an undercooked meal at a restaurant, you would send it back to the kitchen for completion. Go back to God so He can complete you and fill the voids in your life. A relationship with God is the only relationship that will guarantee success and fulfillment in your life. God is the main ingredient. After all, who wants to experience anything without the main ingredient?

On the other hand, if you know that you have the main ingredient, you're definitely hot and ready!!! Continue to pursue God. Be encouraged, because He's on the way! There is nothing like being hot and ready when your husband finds you.

The weariness of waiting

It can be frustrating when people think that because you're single, something must be wrong with you. If you have found yourself in obedience to God, know that there is nothing wrong with you. God has the perfect time set aside for you to get married, and He has not forgotten about you. He's working on you and your husband to get you both in alignment with His will. As you both stay in God's will, it's only a matter of time until you will meet each other and know that this is God aligning you. This is why you have to stay focused on God's will for your life. God is trying to guide you into the right place. Don't miss God because you choose your will and your way. Your will is not big enough and doesn't always consider the plans God has for you. Your will sets you on a completely different path. Work with God and not against Him. You must desire His perfect will. So if a relationship doesn't work out, know that God is only protecting you from even more damage it might give you in the future. It's not God's desire for you to be experimented on and treated like someone on the side. Be confident and love yourself enough to want to wait for God's best.

Know that God has graced you for this season in your life. According to 2 Corinthians 12:9 KJV, "And he said unto me, My grace is sufficient for thee: for my strength is made perfect in weakness. Most gladly therefore will I rather glory in my infirmities, that the power of Christ may rest upon me." God's grace is all you need for this season and for every season. You may feel frustrated in being single, but know that God has provided His grace. His grace will carry you when you're at the lowest point in your life. It will allow you to keep moving forward in the midst of disappointments. It will provide the strength you never knew you had and give such a peace that you can't explain. Grace keeps you humble and reminds you that you can do nothing without God. It's only because of His grace that you will have the strength and the ability to overcome this season. So don't say, "*If* I make it through this season." Say, "*When* I make it…!" Begin to change your confession as you gain perspective. Change how you think about your singleness and the negative things that are attached to it. You will overcome and come out of this season, if you believe it. God has graced you, so you got this! Remember, it's just a season, and seasons always change.

CHAPTER 2

Preparing for the Challenges

As a single, dedicated Christian, I began to do things God's way. I came to the liberating understanding of allowing God to take control of my life; I learned to be at peace with the path and purpose of my life. It ultimately led me to be at the right place at the right time for my husband to find me. Even though God sent me the man of my dreams, I wasn't truly ready for him like I thought I was. Now that I am 13-plus years into my marriage, I think about what I could have done to better prepare myself for marriage. Ladies, we must admit one simple truth: Many of the examples or principles we were exposed to growing up may not work. I have watched my parents because they have been married my entire life. After observing their marriage, I thought I would be prepared for marriage. Unfortunately, this was not the case.

Nothing really prepares you for the dark, disappointing, and embarrassing moments you may face in your marriage. You're not always prepared for the truth or betrayal. You never think it will happen to you, and you don't know what to do or who to tell. You never realized how alone you could feel because you have to mask your emotions and what you're going through. Most people can't handle the raw reality of the trials marriages go through. Not only do you have to watch your response, you also have to deal with the response of your husband and how he manages his emotions. How you both deal with stress will draw you closer or drive a wedge between you. The different dynamics can be overwhelming. The shame and embarrassment lead wives to isolation, and many don't get the professional counseling they need. They then become bitter and angry. These are some of the reasons some wives seem to be so mean and always have an attitude. Some wives wish they'd waited for someone better and regret the decisions they made in choosing their husbands.

Being married and working with other married couples, I realized many of the challenges we face are very similar; we seem to all go through the same phases. While some of the things I am going to share with you may scare you or cause you to question whether you should get married, that's not the message you should get from this book. The aim of this book is to better prepare you to avoid these mistakes so you won't be blindsided and think there's something wrong with your marriage. This is another reason I wrote this book – so you will know what to do. It takes many years for couples to understand how to work through these challenges. Because so many wives don't know what to do, they are ready to give up and throw their marriage away. By understanding the challenges before you get married, you'll have that head start many marriages never have.

Why are couples divorcing?

Many couples are getting married and divorced like it's just another relationship that didn't work. However, studies have shown that most couples regret getting a divorce. They realize, in hindsight, that divorce was the wrong choice. They mistake the issues and brokenness in marriage as something that can't be fixed or restored. Perhaps they don't realize that almost anything that is dealt with early on can be fixed. Marriage is a marathon, not a sprint, and you vowed to be there for better and for worse (not including any form of abuse). You must be committed to the journey/process of becoming and staying as one.

For those who are divorced and single again, I pray God's continuous healing and restoration for all you've lost. No one goes into a marriage to turn around and get a divorce. It's a hurtful process that no marriage should ever have to endure. It truly breaks my heart to see another marriage end, and that's one of the reasons I wrote this book. I wanted to give perspective to those women who desire to marry but are not sure of what it takes to have a successful marriage. Whether you're divorced or never married, I hope this book will bless you.

There are three thoughts I want you to keep in mind as you go through this book. We all must first keep in mind the impact of our past and where we have been. Secondly, we must understand the challenges of where we currently stand. Thirdly, we must grasp an understanding of our past missteps and the stagnation of our current lives. We can all overcome the challenges and pitfalls created by them. We must be aware of the impact our past decisions have made on how we move, think, and consider our future.

Our ineffective communication

The inability to communicate can be one of the greatest hindrances to having a successful marriage. If you grew up in a judgmental or critical environment, you are more than likely carrying hurt and anger. You were never afforded the chance to express yourself; you weren't able to believe or think differently than your parents without feeling condemned. Maybe you grew up in an oppressive home environment where conflict resolution was not taught or practiced. What the head of the house said was law, and you didn't dare to come against it. All you knew was that the wife was not to question the dictates of her husband and was expected to be subservient to him. Without properly learning how to communicate, you'll find it difficult to express yourself.

When you're married and forced to express yourself but don't know how, you become frustrated in trying to be understood. You might either shut down or build a wall with words to shut others out. If this is you, ask God to heal the past wounds and hurt that have controlled your behavior and how you communicate.

You may say you were raised in a single-parent home, and your mother made all the decisions and ran the house. You must unlearn all the controlling behavior you have seen. You do not have to fight for your independence or power in the relationship. You must be trustworthy and wise to operate in your role as a help meet (see Genesis 2:18). As a wife, you're going to want to prevent disasters from happening, but what I have learned is that God allows you to go through different tests and trials that no one can stop; every trial occurs to make you stronger.

> *"My brethren, count it all joy when ye fall into divers temptations; Knowing this, that the trying of your faith worketh patience. But let patience have her perfect work, that ye may be perfect and entire, wanting nothing"*
> **(James 1:2-4 KJV)**

> *"That the trial of your faith, being much more precious than of gold that perisheth, though it be tried with fire, might be found unto praise and honour and glory at the appearing of Jesus Christ"*
> **(1 Peter 1:7 KJV)**

"But the God of all grace, who hath called us unto his eternal glory by Christ Jesus, after that ye have suffered a while, make you perfect, stablish, strengthen, settle you"
(1 Peter 5:10 KJV)

Know that things are going to happen in your marriage, and blaming your husband or tearing him down with your words will cause more damage to your marriage. In your emotional frustration, you may say things that can never be taken back. A man will always remember how you treated him when he was down, and when things get better, he will have a lower level of appreciation for you. Then you will have to take time to repair all the damage you caused.

You must learn to walk in love and continued forgiveness. This is why it's so important to marry someone who is saved and has a heart for God. If he knows how to love God, he will know how to love you. This will help you avoid some of the risks of being hurt and abused in your marriage. Remember, your husband is a gift from God; be gentle and patient in your communication with him.

Our willingness to listen to understand

When you have a disagreement, listen to understand the other side before being so quick to prove your point. Your point does not matter if you don't understand what's happening. Listen for the real issue. Let him talk long enough to tell you the root of the problem. Sometimes men just want to talk without being judged, accused, or interrupted. You must learn to control your emotions. Then he will want to come to you and no one else. It's a bad feeling to learn something about your husband that he felt he couldn't tell you. You want to be his safe place where he can tell you the good, the bad and the ugly without you going crazy as a result. He is a real man with real challenges, coming to you for help. There is no good or easy way for him to say that he has thoughts of cheating, but before he can even express his challenges, most women have kicked him out of the house. He only wanted to tell you about his temptation and not his fall. When you have a prayer life, you will know exactly what to do. Don't think the worst or get low self-esteem. The fact that he told you lets you know that he doesn't want to keep anything from you. Most of the time, when a man confesses his temptation, it isn't easy because he is exposing himself. Pray him through and love him through it. Let me be clear: I am not saying for a man to cheat. What I am saying is that if he comes to you with his temptation, remember that beyond being your husband, he is your brother in Christ. Lift him up in prayer.

This why I always say that marriage is for mature adults. I refuse to allow the devil to come in and tear up my marriage without a fight. I war in the spirit by praying for my husband and the things he must overcome and endure as a man living for God. It's not easy to carry the weight of providing, protecting, fathering, making decisions, giving you what you need, and the many other responsibilities men have.

One of the greatest blessings you can give to your husband is to build him up with your words. If nowhere else, home should be the place where he gets edified, loved, respected, and supported. You have the ability to give that to him. When you constantly edify him, it can become easier to communicate the issues and improvements that need to be made in the marriage, especially the areas that are difficult to talk about.

You will achieve common ground in how you perceive when you listen to understand, and doing so will help you gain a different perspective. The indication that you have achieved common ground is by how you communicate verbally and physically. You must go beyond compromising and understand why things must be done a certain way. Compromising doesn't work when your nonverbal communication doesn't line up with your words. Most of our communication is nonverbal. Your body language and demeanor may prove that you're not in 100 percent agreement with the compromise. Most of the time, our perspective is wrong because we look through our painful past experiences.

Making everything all about you will cause your marriage to fail. Take a few minutes to answer the following questions.

1. Are you always right and want things your way?
2. Are you one who doesn't want to be inconvenienced?
3. Are you one who doesn't want to change and only sees things your way?
4. Are you the one who doesn't consider others?
5. Are you controlling or dominating?
6. Do you complain about everything?
7. Do you demand attention?

8. Are you defensive or insecure?

9. Are you petty?

10. Do you honestly believe the world revolves around you?

If you answered "yes" to any of these questions and don't change, your marriage could be over before it really starts. This is not to make you feel bad about yourself, but to be exposed. This is the time to be honest about where you are and to make changes. Prior to marriage, I could answer yes to six of those questions, so there is no shame here. All of these issues were exposed early on in my marriage. I was embarrassed because I thought I had it all together. I was ready to change. God showed me that change started with my perspective.

If a man marries someone like this, eventually he will get frustrated and begin to check out emotionally and mentally. If a married woman has only one of these characteristics, there will be issues in the marriage. These traits may work if you're single and have no desire to get married. It's like you're in a relationship all by yourself; however, this attitude will destroy a marriage.

The solution to this problem is to have the mindset of a servant. When you're serving, it takes the focus off you, and you don't consider the sacrifice that is required. You no longer keep up with what is being given to you and only responding if you have been served. You begin to anticipate needs and meet them for your spouse. You always pay attention to the details. As a wife, one of your goals is to out-serve your spouse. This will make him feel that you purposed to make him a priority in what you do for him. I would only suggest that you serve him in this way once you are married. You can do very little while dating. When he marries you, this will be one of his benefits.

One of the biggest failures in a marriage, out of all I previously mentioned, is not being willing to change. Your spouse sees you in ways you can't. This issue will cause a spouse to give up on you and the marriage because when you don't want to change, it's like punching a brick wall. You will never tear down a wall when you can only punch it and aren't allowed to use any other tools. That wall will never come down; your painful and bloody knuckles will prove that it's not worth the fight. You can only fight resistance for a short period of time before you decide to give up. This is why the next chapter is so important and will begin to prepare you for marriage. I would even say that the next chapter is the most important one in the book, and if you miss this part, you missed my whole intention. Please hear my heart and remember that we all have to strive to become the wife our husband is going to need.

CHAPTER 3

I'm Ready!

Under construction…Fix "it" now or pay for it later

My husband and I are in the real estate business. When we flip a house, we want to get an inspection first to see what's wrong with the house. Most importantly, we want to know if there are any issues with the foundation. Next, we look at the numbers to see if the project will be profitable and if we should continue with the purchase of that property. Once we do our due diligence, we purchase the property and work on the project until it is complete and ready to be put on the market. This is exactly what we are going to do in this chapter. You will do your own personal inspection – your own due diligence – and work on yourself until you're ready to be put on the market.

You will learn about your identity, counterfeits, attracting the right one, and so much more.

Do "you" while you can

This is not the time to sit around at home doing nothing all day. Get out and go where you want to go while you still can. Most women, after they get married, want to go on trips and have nights out with their girlfriends, and they get angry when their husbands ask them to stay home. If your husband needs you home, then you may want to stay home. Your husband may not tell you that he's tempted to go out and hook up with another woman so he won't be lonely; he may just ask you to stay home. Don't get me wrong, I have girlfriends that I spend time with, but I love hanging with my husband, and he is my best friend. I am talking about wives who act like they're single and don't want to be questioned about anything. They don't feel that they need to be accountable to their husbands, but you both need to be accountable to each other when you're married. You have to talk things through with your husband to be in agreement with whatever you're trying to do. For example, you may want to go back to school, and he may feel like it's not the right time. You have to consider how he feels, like he has to consider how you feel. So, get all of that out of your system. Get up and go while you can! Have some fun!

Don't stay focused on being lonely and not being married. This is the time to begin to perfect yourself. If I could go back, I would have worked more on myself. Marriage exposed my flaws, and I didn't realize how much work I still needed to do. The light will shine on you, and your husband sees it all. Below are some things you may want to work on while you're waiting. These are some of the biggest issues and concerns that come with marriage. You don't want to be working on these when you're already married, like most wives. Get ahead of the game and have your stuff together. You will thank me later!

Begin by writing out the areas where you need help. Study/read books to master these areas and then get to work.

» Spending Money: Master budgeting and stop living beyond your means. For example:

Monthly Income: 15% Tithes and Offering/Gifts, 15% Savings, 40% Invest, 30% Budget and Bills. So, if you need a monthly budget of $3,000 a month to live on and cover all of your bills, your monthly income should be at least $10,000.

» Health: Eat right and exercise. Take care of yourself, so your husband can enjoy you and not be forced to take care of you.

» Decision-making: Know what you want, and have your own perspective. Be able to make a decision when your husband needs you to do so.

» Build endurance: Be patient in the process. There will be times when you want to give up on communicating and trying to work on your marriage. There will always be something to work on in your marriage, and you can't put a time limit on when these issues will be resolved. Always remember that marriage is a marathon, not a sprint. This type of patience will help you build a strong solid marriage.

» Work through the challenges: Learn how to maneuver through your obstacles. You must learn how to be committed beyond personal benefit. Don't be so easy to give up when you don't get your way.

» Petty behaviors: These include needing revenge or

being selfish. This will cause your husband to not take you seriously, because he will see you like a child he is raising instead of his wife. This behavior is not of a wife and is frustrating for a husband to have to deal with. Your husband needs you to be mature, to help him and not embarrass him.

» Personal goals: What are 10 things you would love to have accomplished before marriage? Some examples are homeownership, a degree, investments, being debt-free. This is what you bring to the table; better yet, have your own table. You should never need a husband in order to pursue your goals. There are many other single women doing big things. We work with single-mom investors all the time. You can work on investing most of your income and multiplying what you have, and it will eventually replace your current income. Don't make any excuses; find a way to accomplish your goals.

Your identity

Many women get into a relationship and completely lose their identities. They immerse themselves in the life and lifestyle of whoever they are dating. I remember being with someone who smoked marijuana all the time. In my desire to spend as much time with him as possible, I picked up his habit of smoking marijuana daily as well. I thank God that I never got addicted, but assimilating to his daily habit was outside of my character. However, I was only about what he wanted to do, regardless of my personal objections and principles. In many other relationships, I lost time, my purpose and motivations by waiting. I would sit by the phone waiting to get a call, text, or some type of communication. My world would stop; I never wanted to make any plans, just in case the person of my affection wanted to spend time with me. I was always available and ready whenever they called. When it was time to go our separate ways, I hated living life without them. I didn't have any hobbies or goals to achieve. Having a man was my number one priority and the only thing on my mind. When I was without a man, I was extremely lonely and depressed. Thank God social media wasn't around back then, because I would probably be a wreck.

After salvation and committing to God, I was able to create a life that would be pleasing to Him. I realized that I did not know who I really was or what I had an interest in, so I thought about some activities I loved to do and made them my hobbies. Then I set my top five priorities in life. This helped me maintain a balance and keep the things that were most important to me as a part of my weekly schedule. I found the real me and began to live a better, emotionally stable, and healthier life.

Before we move on, make sure you know yourself and what's important to you. What do you love to do more than anything? Are you allowing time in your schedule for the things that are most important to you?

Take this time to answer the questions below.

1. Who are you (characteristics)?

_____

_____

2. What are you striving to be?

_____

_____

3. What do you like the most about yourself?

_____

_____

4. What are your hobbies?

   a. _____ _____

   b. _____

   c. _____

4. What are your priorities?

(example: God, family, church/ministry, career, health)

   a. _____

   b. _____

   c. _____

   d. _____

   e. _____

It will be ideal if you can complete this before you enter a relationship. Begin living a life of happiness and fulfillment now. It's important for you to create a life that pleases God; your spouse is a bonus and adds to what you have going on. This will be a perfect time to really get to know yourself. Take a vacation to really learn about yourself.

Counterfeits vs. The Real

Two months before I met my husband, the guy I was dating broke up with me. I was left feeling devastated and did not understand why things fell apart. It really seemed like the perfect relationship. Up to that point, I hadn't had a relationship where the guy I was dating wanted marriage. At that time, he was in the military, had his own house, car, and a great personality. He was respectful and always wanted to make me happy. Everything seemed just right – or so I thought. The issue with a counterfeit is that it looks like the real thing. Since he had a desire to marry me, I thought he was the one. I really thought God had sent him to me, but God was trying to show me all the signs of how he was not the one. These were signs I did not want to see. We didn't serve the same God, and he was very inconsistent. There were times when he would ask to take me out but didn't show up. He would then call three days later with an explanation for why he hadn't shown up and didn't call or text. There were so many excuses, and I began to see a pattern whenever it was time for us to go out on a date. I overlooked it, and I wanted to believe he was telling me the truth. When it was time to meet my parents, he never showed up. Then he made another excuse, saying something came up. It doesn't matter how little the excuses are; when it is a continuous pattern, it is a clear sign of inconsistency and that there may be something wrong in the relationship.

I later found out that he was connecting with a woman from his past; it was his inability to look beyond his past that eventually led to our breakup. As I look back, I can see all the warning signs and red flags. I overlooked the signs that were in front of me. At the time, I refused to see the truth because this was a man who said he wanted to marry me.

You may be in a relationship or about to enter a relationship where the man is talking marriage, and you want to believe he is the one. Ladies, be aware of the warning signs and know that God will not send you just anyone. Don't be so desperate to get married that as soon as he says "marriage," you become blinded by the reality of what you're about to really get yourself into.

What's going to attract and keep the right one?

My husband and I had a conversation one day, and he began to share with me what really attracts a man of God to a woman of God. He shared that a woman's worship and commitment to God is very attractive. This is why I stress that your walk with Christ has to be authentic. You can't fake true worship. A man of God wants you to really be saved. Not perfect, but someone who loves God to where she won't compromise or do anything that will disconnect her from the Father. Your love for God must be real. Men also love it when you're confident about how you look. You may not think you're beautiful, but to him, you are. You may not understand what he sees in you that makes him want to pursue you. All you need to know is that a man of God will only have eyes for you. I believe God puts that attraction to you in him so he will know who to pursue. It's all a part of God's plan.

If you're going to keep him, you must stay true to who you are and not compromise your relationship with God. Keep your focus on God, and continue to draw closer to Him. Your relationship with God should never change because you begin to date someone or get married. Even after I got married, I still made sure to spend time with God daily, to continue to maintain my relationship with Him. I am a better wife only because of my prayer life. I am who I am because of God and the relationship we have. Don't get me wrong; I love my husband very much, but I love God more. Let me be clear: I am not saying ignore your husband, but learn to have balance.

A man has to feel like he needs you and that you would add to him. When dating, you should never feel like you cannot fully enjoy life or function without the man you are in a relationship with. Never be addicted to that relationship to the point that if it ever ended, you would feel like you were broken, depressed, and don't have anything else to live for. That is a true sign of codependency and is very unhealthy for a relationship. It will also run a man off because you put him in the place of God. In a sense, you are holding him responsible for your happiness. There are some things we can only get from God, and happiness is one of them.

When you are in a relationship and things do not work out, it is not an indication that you aren't being worthy of being in a relationship. You don't need a relationship to validate you.

Do not lose your confidence. Always remember, he is not the one and be at peace with the relationship coming to an end. You are perfect for the man God has for you; he will know it and never want to let you go. The perfect one for you will actually work hard to make sure your relationship is successful and healthy.

Have you ever noticed how fast a man gets married when he finds the woman he feels is the one? This is not just saved men but men who seem to have sworn off any interest in marriage. Then God reveals to him that she is the one and put such urgency in his heart to make sure he doesn't lose her. He will no longer be afraid of commitment, and he will embrace a future with her. This is how a man can be in a relationship with someone for a very long time and feel unsure about marriage but then finds the right one and becomes totally convinced that she is going to be his wife. He may be unsure toward the beginning of the relationship, but it should never go on for a long period of time. When his unsure for a long time, it's normally a result of having no boundaries or standards in place, and you begin to have sex in the relationship. The man either quickly marries you because he wants to do things right, or he tries to avoid the marriage conversation because he doesn't see himself married to you and needs to buy more time.

Trust me, there's a clear difference between them both. Most women (including me) have a hard time believing that such love really exists. Before my husband, I never experienced a man who was willing to fight for our relationship and really wanted a future with me. It all sounded good, but I didn't believe it was actually possible. I thought some women were just blessed and ended up with a good man. I didn't fully understand that those men had two things the man I'd been dating (before my husband) didn't have. Most of them had a true relationship with God, and they were looking for a wife. Most of the men from my past did not have a relationship with God, and they definitely were not looking for a wife. It is so frustrating when you know that you're wife material, but for some reason, they just don't see it. Now I know they don't see it because they were never looking for it. I just didn't know it at the time. I thought if I gave the relationship time and patience, then he would see that I was definitely the one for him.

Now looking back, I understand that none of them were connected to my future; none of them would have the ability to pray me through my challenges, and none of them had the patience to understand where I was going in God. My husband is truly meant for me and is built in a way where he can handle the anointing that is on my life. He challenges me to be excellent and to maximize my potential. God knew what I needed, and when I was ready, my husband found me. God truly gave me His best; that's why it's so easy for me to submit, respect and honor my husband. I don't mind him leading me, because I know he's following God. That's why he is worth me serving and making sure his needs come before mine.

The ministry we call marriage is a very important ministry a woman can take on. It's why you can't just marry anybody; growing weary of loneliness and being single are the absolute worst reasons to get married. I want to encourage you to trust God to give you a husband beyond your wildest dreams. God's timing is perfect. More than God's perfect timing, He knows when you are ready. Don't settle, and do not rush into a lifelong commitment.

Why am I still single?

If I can be honest in this section, I will just share the revelation God has given me, for some of you who don't understand why you are still single. If you feel this section isn't for you, please keep reading anyway, and maybe you can share this revelation with someone else. Here are just a few reasons some women are still single.

1. It could be that it's not God's timing, but the enemy will try to make you think there is something wrong with you.

2. It could be that you're not in position to be found. Your husband may be looking for someone who is going after everything God has for her. Most men of God want to add to what you already have and see that it aligns with the vision God has for him. He probably can't find you because you're hidden. Your spiritual gifts and talents are hidden because you have put everything on hold until you get a man.

3. It could be that you can't manage your current responsibilities, and you feel burned out. I mentioned earlier that marriage is a ministry. Servanthood and

faithfulness are at the core of what it means to be married. If you cannot be faithful in small things like church attendance, being a disciple-maker or diligent in ministry assignments, why would God put more on your plate? God is practical and wise; He knows that if you cannot handle the responsibilities of ministry for a few hours a week, then you definitely cannot handle the responsibilities of marriage, which is a 24-hour ministry. An indication that you're not ready for more responsibilities is when you are not asked or considered for anything extra. It means that you are in a season of preparation; in other words, you must first learn to master where you are before more is added. There is nothing wrong with being prepared. This is when you should take advantage of working on yourself.

Take the time to examine your attitude, heart, and motivations for serving in your local ministry and in the community. Serving is the key, but the most important facet of serving is your attitude. The heart of a true servant is serving without wanting anything in return. If you can identify and meet the needs in your local church and community, you will easily identify the needs in your marriage. Many Christians do not understand their responsibility in making disciples. Christians must build other disciples by watching what they are saying and modeling the correct behavior. You would be surprised at how many people are watching how you handle challenging situations. You must desire to be the best example for other singles. In some cases, the precedent and example you display will be the one modeled by others when they face the same challenges, concerns, and dilemmas. What will other singles learn from you? Will you be proud of the example you set or embarrassed when you see the behavior you displayed mirrored in others?

I know this is a tough section, but please hear my heart. Waiting for my husband was one of the most challenging and frustrating times I've ever experienced. So trust me, I understand. I gave and still give my all in my local church, and when my husband found me, I was busy for the Lord. God wants to use you in your singleness. He needs your time and talent. He didn't save us to get married, but to be about His business, The Great Commission.

4. Another reason may be that you haven't mastered your flesh. Not just sexually, but the war with your flesh. You must learn how to win the battle in your mind, will, and emotions, which all affect your flesh. I remember there were seasons in my singleness that were harder than normal with my thoughts and physical desires. I have learned that a season may last one day, one week, or a few weeks. I had thoughts that tried to put me into a state of depression and doubt. I felt a strong desire for companionship and the attention of a man. During that time, I remember not watching much TV but spending more time in prayer so I could fight against the warfare that was coming against me. Sometimes, I would stay in prayer until I fell asleep. With many tears, I would stay before the Lord until I got my peace. Now looking back, I realize God was making a warrior out of me. God knew the trials that were ahead of me, and He was preparing me to go through anything.

Now, you would think that marriage makes life easier, but the truth is that you're entering another level of testing and trials. Marriages are meant to display God's glory. Marriage will show you how spiritually mature you are and how much faith you have. Your flesh is always going to want to win, and pride will cause your marriage to fail, in which Satan gets the victory. God wants to show you how marriage can work and what He's able to do with two individuals who love and obey Him. Your marriage is not about curing your loneliness and sexual needs; it's about going through the fire and coming out like gold. Your marriage is not going to be perfect, but God will grace you for your spouse. God will bring you joy and happiness in the midst of a storm. Marriage is not a fairy tale; that's why you vow to be there for better or for worse. This is not to scare you, but to be honest with you. As I said before, I am happily married, and it's only by God's grace. He will grace you, but you must be willing to love and obey Him.

Becoming a wife

The woman in Proverbs 31:10-31 had to marry a man who would support and know how to lead a strong woman who knows how to flow in everything God has graced her to be. She had to know where God was taking her, and that not just any man would work. I don't believe she became virtuous once she got married, but rather when her husband found her as a virtuous wife already. When your husband finds you, he finds you as a wife already. "Whoso findeth a wife findeth a good thing, and obtaineth favour of the LORD" (Proverbs 18:22 KJV). This may be a challenge for some women, not understanding what a wife really is.

How can you properly get ready for something when you don't really know what you're getting ready for? Unless you have been married before, you can't really know. Nothing and no one really prepares you for what you will face or endure once you are married. Some married women may give you advice, but truth be told, we're still working to become better wives and continuously learning from our mistakes. When married women tell you to "wait on God," what they are saying is that marriage is very serious. It's more serious than they thought, and they understand the temptation to settle. They understand the pain and disappointment that comes with settling. In all honesty, married women do not want single women to endure the unnecessary warfare that comes with being ill-prepared or choosing the wrong spouse. Future wives must understand that the encouragement to wait is a call to be cautious. Married women want your marriage to be a peaceful and positive experience, and this can only happen if you receive who God intended for you. Your husband is a gift from God. Gifts bring joy, a level of fulfillment, and validation, but they also require work and maintenance.

Waiting for who God has for you really makes a difference in the type of marriage you will have. Remember, you can follow God's way or your own way; He will honor it, either way. On the other hand, there are unnecessary challenges that come with doing things your own way. Ultimately, I encourage you to run from the counterfeit, because the real one is on the way. I will talk more about counterfeit relationships later on. I want you to know I absolutely love being married. I thank God for giving me the grace to wait for my husband to find me.

Am I ready for marriage?

Here are 10 questions to ask yourself. Write your answers in your journal.

1. Do you want a spouse, or do you want a companion?

There is a big difference between the two. In all actuality, many women are tired of being alone and desire more of a companion than a spouse. Do you only want to be married because you want to avoid the potential of him leaving you for someone else and because you love the time and attention he gives you when he's around? In this case, marriage may seem like the right thing to do. I understood this line of thinking, because that is what I thought made a happy marriage (always wanting to be together). I loved the phone calls and the attention. I liked the idea of being the only one on his mind. After a few years of being married, I realized that we don't agree on certain things; we want our own space at times, and even in a marriage, you can still feel alone. So, companionship was not enough for my marriage.

Being a spouse is more of being committed in tough times and staying when you want to leave. It's loving him beyond his failures, bad habits, and negative attitudes, some of which you will never really experience until after you're married. Life can throw all kinds of things your way, and your husband may not know how to cope with them. This is when you may see a different side of him, a side no one else has ever seen, and you must love him through it. Always remember to not take everything personally, because men have a hard time expressing how they are feeling. The worst thing you can do is to make it all about you. He will be tempted to find someone, maybe another woman, who will listen, help, love, and support him. If you're not willing to be a spouse (listen, love, help, and support him), no matter how rough things get, then you just want a companion.

    a. Companion

    b. Spouse

    c. Not sure

2. What is your temperature spiritually? (see Revelations 3:15-16)

    » If you're hot, then your trust is in God that He will bring you a man of God when you're ready for him, and you are at peace with that.

    » If you're lukewarm, you're frustrated while you wait on God and keep a negative attitude. You're probably offended with God. You may feel like God is giving you this desire and doesn't plan to bring it to pass. You even may slip up and have sex occasionally, but really desire to do things God's way and keep yourself holy. It's a struggle because you're hot sometimes and cold other times.

» If you're cold, you want what you want, and you want it now. You consistently attract the wrong guy or believe that he will change with time. You're not on fire for God, and He doesn't have the opportunity to be Lord in your life.

If you were to be honest, are you hot, lukewarm, or cold?

a. Hot

b. Lukewarm

c. Cold

3. Are you ready to die to self?

As a wife, you're going to be inconvenienced, tired, and selfish at times. You must always think of yourself as "we," not "me." Marriage a lifetime of serving him and compromising. If you're spoiled, like I was, and don't like to be inconvenienced, then wait until you're ready to change that about yourself before you even start dating. You don't want him not marrying you because you're not willing to give up the "me" for "we." A man of God will be turned off by your selfishness and will disqualify you, when all you have to do is change. On the other hand, if you just love to serve and always put the needs of others before your own, then some men don't deserve you and won't appreciate you. Make sure he's worth it and be willing to put your needs before his. Both of you should die to self, not just one of you (Romans 12:1-2, Galatians 2:20, Luke 9:23-24, Romans 8:12-13).

    a. Ready to change

    b. Not ready

    c. Don't need to change

4. Are you prepared for what you want in a husband (equal standards)?

    If you have high standards for him and low standards for yourself, it is not fair. Or what if he is a man of God, but hasn't accomplished much? As long as he has a plan and a strong prayer life, he is going to do some great things and be all God has called him to be.

If you do know what you want, but have never dated anyone on that level, you will need to know if you will be able to handle all that comes with that man. Sometimes we love what we see and all the accomplishments that come with him, but don't realize the discipline, sacrifice, and stressed lifestyle that's attached to it. A man (any man) needs a prayer warrior as a wife. Are you willing to fast and pray him through every area of his life?

It's trendy to live an entrepreneurial lifestyle or be married to someone wealthy. What many women don't realize is that until a company is built or the wealth is built, the husband may spend most of his time working. In this case, you may feel as if his work comes before you. You may hit a rough patch financially because of the different seasons in the business. Unless your parents built a business or wealth, you're probably wanting a lifestyle that you don't understand or can't handle. You're just in love with the idea and how it looks. Or you may want to marry someone in the military, but never considered the deployments and the many times you will have to relocate because of his military career. Some women can handle it, and some can't. So, for whatever you desire in a husband, make sure you're willing to accept all that comes with him.

Before I met my husband, I believed I would marry someone who was destined for greatness. After I met him, I knew he was who I wanted but I still didn't know what all came with him. Marrying him has caused me to come up in all my weak areas to be the help God created me to be. When you get married, all of your weaknesses are exposed, and you must be willing to improve in those areas. A strong prayer life, humility, and patience helped me to overcome my weaknesses. I am still working on some of my weaknesses after 13-plus years of marriage, and this is why it's important to be patient.

    a. I know what I want, but I'm not sure what it will be like married to someone on that level.

    b. I know what I want and can handle it.

    c. I know what I want, but I realize that I need to come up in some areas to be able to nurture and help my husband at this level.

    d. I don't really know what I want, but I trust God and His plan.

5. Are you in position to receive that man?

Make sure you're healed and restored from your past relationships. This means you forgive, release, and let them and the pain go. Then you won't see your new relationship with the same lens of your past. Are you in position?

a. Yes

b. No

6. Is Jesus Lord over your life?

When you allow Jesus to be Lord, you're obedient to His word. You allow Him to lead and guide you in the direction He wants you to go. This will help when you get married and want to be submissive to your husband. Allow God to lead you and be in control, which will require you to trust Him in all things. Is God in control?

a. Yes

b. No

c. Sometimes

7. Are you in a relationship with God?

When you're in a relationship, you take time to learn more about them and to see what's in their heart. You learn what they like and don't like. You learn how to communicate, how to listen, and how to love them.

   a. Yes

   b. No

8. Do you have a strong prayer life? It's important to pray at least once a day to examine yourself and to get direction from God. You should pray when you need healing, deliverance and a renewed mind. Prayer gives you comfort and peace. Have you been consistent in prayer?

   a. Yes

   b. No

9. Is your spirit man strong? When you feed (with prayer and studying the word of God) the spirit man, it gets stronger. You'll know that your spirit man is stronger when you resist temptation and guard yourself from fulfilling the flesh (sinful nature).

a. Yes

b. No

10. Were you honest in all of your answers?

It's important to be honest with where you are in your walk with Christ. If these areas aren't exposed now, they will be exposed in your marriage. These questions will help you see what kind of foundation you have. You must make sure that your foundation (the basics of Christianity) is solid. So, when your husband finds you, your foundation is right. Nobody wants a house with foundation issues, and that is the same with a man of God.

a. Yes

b. No

CHAPTER 4

Your First YES!

Different levels of commitment (Your "YES" to God)

There are different phases you will go through as you mature and grow in your relationship with Christ. These phases help you identify your current commitment level.

The "teenage love" phase: In this phase, you're not saved and need to repent. You may think and say that you are saved. You may be like teenagers, who think they know everything, do whatever they want to do, and do not want God to be Lord over them. You may be rebellious at times.

The "we're talking" phase: You get saved, but you're not willing to let go of your sin. Your heart is divided; you have the form of godliness, but no power. You want a little bit of God and a little bit of the world. You're not sure you really want to be in a relationship with God.

The "dating" phase: When you first get saved, you begin to tell people about God. This is also the time you're getting to know Him. He will begin to reveal the revelation of His word, and this keeps you excited and wanting more of Him.

The "lukewarm relationship" phase: Over time, you begin to stray and aren't sure where the relationship is going. You're not sure that you trust God anymore. Someone else may be in your ear or have your attention. Sometimes you're in, and sometimes you're out. Sometimes you're ashamed of serving Christ, because it's not trending, and you love Him in secret. You're not sure of what you want.

The "engagement" phase: You decided to say yes to God. You made it through the tough, lukewarm times and decided that this is it for you, and you will serve Him for the rest of your life. He will give you eyes to see and ears to hear His voice. Revelation from God is flowing, but the enemy temps you because he knows you're still growing, and if you don't keep a strong prayer life, you can still back out at any time.

The "ceremony/commitment" phase: This is when God really has your yes! There's no turning back. You then get to the heart of God (caring about what HE cares about). Your highest desire is to live a lifestyle that pleases Him. You begin to tap into your purpose, allowing God to be Lord over you, through obedience and humility. You serve diligently in your local church and community.

You're at a place where you only say "yes" when God asks you to do something because you are one with God, and you know His heart. Things that hurt Him also hurt you, and you will be led to pray about it. You're letting the work He started in you be completed. You trust in God and whichever way He takes you.

Marriage requires you to be saved for real. You must have the nature and mindset of Christ.

So, are you ready? Here is how to position yourself to be found.

#1 Receive Christ as your personal Lord and Savior, which means that you're in a relationship with Him.

#2 Allow that relationship to grow, and learn to listen and follow His voice. Develop your relationship with God.

#3 Develop a servant's heart.

#4 Continue to be obedient to God and let patience perfect you.

#5 Learn to continuously forgive and give grace.

#6 Deal with your root issues and be healed from them.

#7 Become the best you.

#8 When it's all done, get a makeover! Let the outside match the inside.

CHAPTER 5

My Process

I learned early in life that everything wrong or the things I was unhappy about started with me and my decisions. I understood that what I did and didn't do affected me. Before I received Jesus Christ as my Lord and Savior, I found myself in dead-end relationships. At the time, I didn't realize they were going nowhere. I'd give all I had in those relationships, leaving me with little to give once my husband actually found me. I was backsliding when I first met my husband. I remember feeling that if we didn't work out, I wasn't sure I had anything left to give anyone else. My heart had been broken many times since I was 11 years old because I always threw all my focus and energy into my relationships. Being in a relationship was something I felt like I needed, and it made me feel wanted and validated.

I always went to church and knew of God, but I didn't live a surrendered life to Him. When I really decided to make Him my Lord and Savior, my whole life changed. I began to have a deep relationship with God, and He began to show me who I really was. Overall, I was perceived as a good girl. Most people saw me as a polite, sweet and young woman who was focused on her goals. Truthfully, I was focused on being in a relationship and had a lustful/sexual side. I just wanted to please my man and didn't want to be alone. That was my goal and ambition. Nothing else mattered, as long as he was satisfied. Whoever I was dating was the person I couldn't get enough of sexually. At times, I didn't need to be in a committed relationship with him; I just needed him to be available when I needed him. I willfully allowed myself to be used. I put those men before God. I knew if I rededicated my life to Christ, I would lose the man I was with; I felt like I needed him sexually. I created soul ties that were hard to break. The sexual encounters felt so good that I didn't want to give it up, not even for God. I had given up drinking, smoking marijuana, cussing, and clubbing, but I couldn't let go of the sex.

Sex had such a stronghold over my life, and I was a slave to my sin. I knew if I could be delivered from it, I could give God all of me and He could have my whole heart. I no longer wanted to feel like I was addicted to sex as if it was a drug, so I went to a weekend retreat (Women's Encounter) and received the deliverance that I needed. That was when my whole life changed, and I was finally free. I had to close every door that would let the enemy back into my life to cause me to go back to the bondage God had freed me from. I had to learn how to sincerely live for Christ. I had to delete some numbers and cut off every ungodly relationship. When the sexual thoughts came, I had to cast them down. I remember getting rid of porn, sexual toys, and music that made me want to go there sexually. Certain songs made me feel lonely and depressed, so I cut out all worldly music because it was hard for me to be free and listen to the music I was listening to. It seemed as though the music was drawing me more and more away from God at a time when I needed him to be close. It was very hard for me to give up secular music, but when I turned the radio station to the Christian channel, I never turned it back. I began to find Christian music that I loved, and it started to make a huge difference in my thought life. My mind needed to be renewed because most of my life, I'd served the devil, and my thinking was off. I made really bad choices and didn't have any clear direction. After being set free, I did not want to repeat the mistakes of the past.

When I asked God to save me, I wanted to be saved beyond not going to hell. I knew that without Christ, I was destroying my life. I wanted to be saved from myself and the terrible decisions I was making. In my singleness, God told me that if I didn't control my sexual desires then, I wouldn't be able to control them when I got married. God knows some men may look better than your husband or treat you better, and the temptation might be there. Before I got married, I feared I'd be married but desire to be with someone else. I only felt this as the wedding date got closer. By God's grace, I still only desire my husband and no one else. I believe it's because I committed to living holy before God while we dated.

Just to rewind a little; when I first met my husband, I was a backslider (not saved), and we were intimate. I rededicated my life to God, and we went our separate ways. He eventually rededicated his life to the Lord and joined my church. A month later, he met with my pastor to receive counsel about pursuing me in courtship (dating), and my pastor gave his blessings. At that point, we both made the decision to keep our relationship holy. It's easier to live holy when you both desire to do so.

Keeping yourself holy is not just for singles, but while you're single, you have the opportunity to learn how to guard yourself against the temptation and master this skill to avoid cheating in your marriage. If you've never had an opportunity to control yourself or build up enough strength to resist the temptation, the devil is waiting for you to get married and to continue to control you. Overcome the temptations of your flesh and be careful with your thoughts.

CHAPTER 6

I Am That Good Thing!

Mastering the dating phase

My husband and I go to a restaurant where the food is amazing and satisfying, but it's not nearby, and it always has a long wait. There's a similar restaurant not far away. It isn't that good, but we go anyway, out of convenience (closer and no wait). We just are not patient enough to get what we really want. This is also what happens when we as women start to date. We waste time and energy entertaining the wrong man. We take too long discerning the direction of the relationship. We want what we want, even if it's not that good. We settle because we are tired of waiting. This is when we miss who God has for us, because of our weariness. I want to encourage you to trust God and His timing, and you will be amazed and satisfied!

What do you need to know before dating?

You may not be married yet, but you must start to see yourself as a wife. Your husband should find you as a wife already, a "good thing" (see Proverbs 18:22). The evidence of a "good thing" is that you become a woman without compromise and with integrity. Compromise could be dangerous and put you in an ungodly cycle. Eventually, it will be very difficult to break free from it. It seems small at first but later turns into a monster. Many times, we wake up and think, "How did I get here?" I personally experienced compromise when I was single, and it never led me to the altar. I compromised by dating men who were not saved, in hopes that they would become saved. At times, I made my standards low just so I wouldn't scare him away by wanting to be in a serious, committed relationship. I wasn't honest with him, and I wasn't being true to myself. Only when I began to have standards, boundaries and didn't compromise was I led to the altar. I became honest with men;

I told them about me dating to see if it led to marriage. I was checking them out, and they were checking me out. I no longer cared if they didn't agree with dating to see if it led to marriage. They needed to know that if it led to marriage, great! And if it didn't, it was okay to end it so we could find who we were created for. God didn't create you for all men; He created you for one man.

I didn't realize that I was becoming a "good thing." A man of God looks for these characteristics (being without compromise and with integrity), and if he's not doing that, I would question his walk with Christ. Outside of your beauty, a man of God wants to know he can trust you and that you wouldn't compromise your relationship with him. You may think you would never do that, but when your relationship is tested, never say what you would never do. I know many marriages and dating relationships where a woman cheats during a difficult time when the relationship is being tested. To be 100 percent honest, when I compromised, I did things I said I'd never do. I'm sure I'm not the only one, right?

Be careful not to compromise your walk with Christ. Watch the way you conduct yourself around other men, such as appearing to be too inviting (body language and conversation). If you notice, most wives with successful marriages are not as inviting with other men (outside of family). They don't engage in deep/emotional conversations with other men. They keep conversations with other men short and to the point. They don't give their phone number to a man but connect him to another man. They shake another man's hand or give him a distant/side hug. They don't look around the room to see if they can make eye contact with someone they're attracted to. They guard themselves against men who are attracted to them, because married women can still find other men attracted. They can't look or think too long about other men, because just like singles, their imagination will go, and they will entertain the thought of being with another man. They must stay guarded!

So, as a single lady, remember that not everyone is welcome to stay in your space. If a man is around you too long, other men will assume you're not available. Know the difference between being found and being entertained. Then, when you're approached by a man, ask yourself, "Which one is he?" Know that a man who wants to entertain you just wants to experiment on you and will ultimately distract you. You will know he's entertaining you by the direction of the conversation. Let him do most of the talking, so you know where he's taking the conversation. Don't tell him what you want in a man; instead, watch to see if he is the man that you want. His actions mean more than what he says, so watch him while you pray to God about him. When you know that you're not being found, be quick to end it and move on before you begin to catch any feelings. You must stay in position to be found, and you will never be found when you are entertaining someone else. When it's time, you want to be found without delay. Don't delay your blessing.

It shows strength and confidence in God when you don't compromise. It allows God to save you from all the unnecessary drama the devil wants you to experience. This is how you will allow God to make you that "good thing" your future husband is looking for. So, be confident in who God created and called you to be. See yourself with unshakable faith in God. See yourself totally surrendered to God and loving Him more than anything. Your worship of God is pure, and your gratitude is expressed in your praise. Being sold out and saved (for real) is the perfect recipe for a wife. It's not all about what you look like on the outside, but the depth you have on the inside.

How do I know he's the husband God sent me?

1. He will be Christ-like and going in the same spiritual direction as you. Since he is Christ-like, he will handle you with care and value. He will respect your walk with Christ and push you closer to Christ.

2. He will not pursue you to defile his or your body in any way (drugs, sex, alcohol, cigarettes, physical abuse). He will seek God and desire to be delivered from these things.

3. He sets boundaries and is willing to guard himself against sexual sin. Remember, what he can't control now, he will struggle with in the marriage. When an opportunity presents itself, he may not be strong enough or able to resist the temptation of another woman. This is practice for marriage. Trust me, you want him to know how to control (guard) his flesh.

4. He is not afraid to get married.

5. He will want to protect you and preserve you.

6. He will bring out the best in you.

7. He will work on how he communicates with you and be willing to share his heart with you.

8. He makes an effort to quickly resolve issues through honest and clear communication.

9. He will be able to trust you with his money, heart, and dreams.

10. He desires a healthy and peaceful relationship.

11. He is willing to provide for and take care of you.

12. He has a prayer life and knows how to obey the voice of the Lord.

At some point when you're dating or engaged, you feel as if you're in love with the man you're with. Once you get married, your love for your spouse will be tested. It's in those moments that you realize what true love really is. It goes beyond a feeling and is shown through your commitment to stand with him no matter what. Just like our love for Christ is tested, so will your love for your spouse.

Stop focusing on what you want and allow God to give you what you need.

I thought I only wanted a good-looking gentleman who adored me, but God knew I needed so much more. At one point, I was actually okay if my husband wasn't a Christian because I didn't understand my purpose. God knew I needed someone with a vision and an excellent work ethic. God knew I needed someone who would not encourage me to be average but would challenge me to be my best in every situation. God gave me far beyond what I was expecting. Where God was taking me required that kind of husband. I clearly see all God intended for me to have in a husband. Since it took years to discover my purpose, there would be no way for me to really know what type of husband I needed. This is why we really need to trust God. Over my many years of marriage, I have grown spiritually, professionally, and mentally because God gave me what I needed and not just only what I wanted.

When I met my husband, he wasn't "my type." We started out as friends, and it grew into love. He was fine, but was nothing like what I was used to dating. After being in so many unhealthy and unbalanced relationships, I didn't know anyone like my husband existed. A lot of married women I know have said the same thing, and you may find yourself in this same situation. It will help if you get a mentor who has the kind of marriage you want as a model for what a healthy relationship looks like. Don't get stuck on "your type," because "your type" may be toxic for you. You will block your blessing if you can only be with a certain type of man. I eventually realized that "my type" was mostly based on appearance and swag. These are what you see on the surface, but I challenge you to go deeper to find all gold that is there. Be open to someone different and not "your type," because he could be the one.

Sometimes we look for what we are not. If you want a man with money, then you need to have some money. If you want him to have a nice house and car, then you should have or be in pursuit of a nice house and car. Before you set all these criteria and standards for a man, make sure you are his equivalent. I'm not saying that you're not worth being with someone who has everything. I'm saying don't pass up someone who may not have all of those material things. He may be in the process of building his business/wealth or furthering his career. Be careful not to demand or require a type of man that you're not willing to be equivalent to.

Don't take the bait!

In the next chapter, I want to discuss your second yes (engagement), but as I mentioned in Chapter 4, your first yes is to God. You must be willing to submit to God before you submit to a husband. Learning first to submit to God will help you stay humble and prepare you to serve in your marriage. It's easier to have your own will and do things your way without considering God. We sometimes have it in our mind what we will and will not do, quite honestly, without considering the word of God and His purpose for our life. We need to stop telling God what we're not going to do. We need to make it a practice and habit to be available to God no matter how much we disagree or how it may inconvenience us.

Before God renewed my mind, there were things I didn't really agree with or understand. Like no sex or living with a man before marriage. I wanted to put my physical needs before God. It felt like there was just a bunch of rules. I have learned that we need to allow God to renew our minds and receive revelation from Him, and then we will see that God only wants to save and protect us. I have learned that nothing good comes out of disobedience.

Pay attention to God's pursuit of you. God wants you and your whole heart. Sometimes we forget God when a man comes into our lives. We cease hearing from God and refuse to allow Him to lead and guide us. Your vision can become cloudy, and you can draw further and further away from God. Before you know it, God has been replaced. Sometimes, God will then have to cause things to happen to get your attention. God wouldn't just allow you to go in the wrong direction without at least trying to intervene. He loves you more than your boyfriend does. Boyfriends will leave you, but God will never leave your side. God forgives you when you mess up and will never throw it back up in your face. Believe that God wants the best for you; He is the only one who knows what you really need.

It is dangerous to get married for reasons beyond God's purpose for your life. Selfish motives linger well beyond the wedding vows. Selfish motives can become hindrances that can destroy a marriage if they are not dealt with correctly prior to marriage. If you find yourself desiring to get married for some, or one, of the motives listed below, slow down and look beyond these factors that can or will change.

1. A ticking biological clock
2. Time invested in a relationship
3. Status/financial security
4. Appearance/attraction
5. Sex
6. Loneliness

When you settle and marry just anybody, you will engage in unnecessary spiritual warfare – especially if it's someone who is not saved and does not have a relationship with God. You're going to want to do things God's way, and he's going to want things his way. You will spend a lot of energy and focus on the attacks instead of being in position to be used by God. Don't delay your spiritual journey just because you want to get married so badly that you settle.

Your husband should be encouraging and supportive of your spiritual growth. You should both continuously mature in your walk with God. Remember that even after marriage, serving God and His people should be high on your priority list. This is where you learn balance for life, family, and work.

Whether you marry the one God has for you or not, you won't avoid spiritual warfare in your marriage. Instead of fighting with your husband, your will fight will be against the demonic. Satan hates marriage and loves to cause division between the two of you; he wants you to fight and blame each other for what is not working in the marriage. For example, you may have communication issues where there is a misunderstanding on both sides. You may have financial or health issues that cause one to blame the other. There could be issues with the kids that are putting a wedge in your marriage. Satan works hard to make sure you are in a state of discord and offense. If Satan can keep you at each other's throats, it will hinder or stop you from having a peaceful and healthy marriage. I remember how it wasn't easy to wait on God, but now I know it was absolutely the best thing for me, my husband, and the success of our marriage.

Bouncing back from a failed relationship

When we get into a relationship, we never want it to fail, and most women work hard to prove themselves in a relationship. Some women think that if they act like a wife, he will want to propose and marry them. Some women think that if they make their man happy, he will stay. Some women think that if they look attractive all the time, then their man won't want anyone else. When a man breaks up with you, it could be for many different reasons. It could have been your fault, or it could be him, but in the end, it doesn't matter. Know that if it is God, it will be, and if it's not, trust God and know that the breakup was for your good. All you can do at this point is continue to work on yourself. Don't focus on being perfect; work on being who God created you to be. Learn from your mistakes and move on. Give yourself a week or two to begin to delete him from your life. Get rid of everything that reminds you of him until he is completely out of your system. Getting him out of your system may take a few months or years, so don't be so quick to jump into another relationship. Pray that God will cut the soul tie you have with him. You don't want to enter into a relationship with someone while you're still thinking about your ex-boyfriend. It will cause you to compare them to each other, which doesn't give the new guy a fair chance. Don't miss the real thing by focusing on the counterfeit.

If you had a bad breakup in a previous relationship and didn't properly bounce back from it, you will carry the hurt into your new relationship. You must be able to reset and start all over again. Here are a few steps you can take to bounce back from any breakup.

1. **Acceptance:** Accept the fact that it's over and let him go. Accept your mistakes and admit the areas where you were at fault. Give all his stuff back, and throw away the things he bought you.

2. **Forgiveness:** Be quick to forgive. Don't be vengeful or petty. Release him.

3. **Learn:** Learn from it. Know what questions to ask next time. Recognize the signs of a dead-end relationship. Recognize the past cycles and break them. Don't become bitter, become better. Live your life like you did before him, because it's not the end of the world.

4. **Time:** Give yourself time to get him out of your system. Allow God to heal your heart (see Psalm 147:3).

Be healed from past relationships, and don't miss your blessing because you aren't ready when God sends him. Before we move on, God wants to cleanse our hearts. He needs us to forgive and release every failed relationship. Let's pray:

I forgive and release _____ (name of ex-boyfriend), and Lord, I ask you to sever every soul tie that still connects me to him. Lord, I release the hurt and feelings of abandonment/ rejection. Remove him from my mind and thoughts. Lord, soften my heart so I don't become bitter. Remove the desire and thoughts of a future with him. Restore every part of me that I lost while I was in that relationship. I ask you, Lord, to give me my confidence back and allow me to see my worth. Help me to never settle again. Give me strength. Continue to prepare and perfect me for my future husband. Heal my heart so I can have the ability to love again and not overlook my future husband when he comes. Lord, I trust you, and I love you with everything that is within me. Even though I hurt right now, I am so grateful that you didn't allow me to make the mistake of marrying the wrong man. I really desire your will and am willing to wait for the man who is meant to be with me. Lord, continue to give me the grace and patience to wait. In Jesus' name, I pray. Amen

CHAPTER 7

Your Second YES!

The engagement

First, let me say congratulations! God is confirming the fact that you are ready to be a wife, and now it is time to implement some very important habits. You should be focusing on respecting and considering him. That means really listening and understanding his perspectives and what motivates him. This is the time you will need to become more of his "help meet" or helper (see Genesis 2:18), knowing and supporting his dreams and goals, praying for his spiritual and professional success. Understand his heart and know that you have a great influence over him that you should never use to manipulate any situations. You no longer have to fight for your independence, because it's not your job to rule over the relationship (and eventually your home).

This is the time where you must work on all selfish habits. You need to get used to things not being about you. You can practice this by focusing more on others around you (family and friends) and meeting some of their needs. You will become sensitive to the needs of others, and it will be easier to implement those habits in your marriage. Start by doing something for someone else that would be a blessing to them or help make their day better. Also, make it a goal to impact a person's life in some way at least once a day. Remember, this only works if you're never expecting anything in return.

There may be times where you're not getting your needs met by your husband and have to meet his needs anyway. You will begin to master this area in your life and become a blessing your husband needs and wants. It will eventually become second nature, in that you purpose to make his life a little easier. You will be inconvenienced and may need to wake up an hour early every day to pray for him and put things in place that may help make his day flow a little better. When you're paying attention to him and sensitive to what he's going through, you will know exactly what to do.

Serving my husband and being sensitive to his needs allows me to be that blessing to him. I learned that getting up early every day to pray for him really helps me hear from God and get wisdom on how to be a better wife. Just because you have him, it doesn't mean the work is done; it's just started. God will continue to make you better if you would allow Him. He will teach you how to be successful in your marriage.

By this point in your journey in this book, you should not be struggling to allow God to change and teach you. That's why it's important to deal with yourself before you get into a relationship with anyone. But if you missed that part of the book, please go back to Chapters 3 and 4.

Some of you have made up in your mind what you will and will not do in your marriage. Set your mind now that you will do all God asks you to do and will be available to be used by Him in your marriage. Don't forget this is ministry you are signing up for, and ministry requires sacrificing your time and giving of yourself. You will be used and may even feel unappreciated. But that's when you remember it's not about you.

Now, the great thing about God is that there is a sowing and reaping principle; you will reap what you sow. Well, guess what? You reap great things. I remember early in my marriage, my husband was continually concerned about my needs and wants. He was driven to do all he could to make life easy and stress-free for me. I noticed that he rarely considered himself. He sowed into me with kind words and sacrificed the things he wanted so he could make sure I was experiencing the blessings that come with being married to him. In many cases, the wife sows more, but in my marriage, my husband was the one who showed me how to sow in a marriage. The more he poured into me, the more I wanted to give back. It got to the point where I constantly thought of different ways to bless him. The more he served me, the more I desired to out-serve him. At this point, we are both reaping! Remember that you may be the first one to do all the serving, but if you don't give up, you will reap in due season.

The reality of marriage: Am I really ready to be a wife?

If you are going into your marriage willing to be a vessel God can use and with a full understanding that this commitment will require a lot of patience and prayer, I would say that you have the potential to be an excellent wife. Prayer will help you have an ear to hear the voice of God, as He is giving you insight and direction on what to say and how to meet your husband's needs. Prayer will cause intimacy. You will grow to love and appreciate your husband more and more every day (love your spouse unconditionally). Prayer also helps us control emotions because they will drive us to do and say things that will bring harm to our marriage.

Let's say you have to continuously learn your spouse and be patient in the areas where he has challenges. Give your spouse time and space to grow beyond where he is. It's okay to allow him to make mistakes. Learning from mistakes and missteps is a vital part of marriage. You'll be able to appreciate your spouse when he begins to mature into an improved version of himself. Always remember, you do not have to be in control of him because you are not his parent, and he is not your child. If this is how you feel going into marriage, it is something you must correct before you say "I do." There are times during a marriage when you will want to take control of a situation, but you have to remember that you are the help meet; you are there to help him make the best decision. Controlling him in every situation will be a quick way to lose him and the man you need him to be.

Also, know that when you are in a disagreement, you do not always have to be right. What good is it for you to win an argument but lose your marriage? Remember to listen to understand (review that section in Chapter 2). Your way is not always the right way. Be quick to check yourself to see if you're wrong. Be very honest and fair. Apologizing is the quickest way to repair any type of damage you may have caused.

Schedule premarital counseling with the pastor who is marrying you or your spiritual covering. They will also help you identify the areas you need to work on. You should also identify a couple who is successful and willing to mentor or counsel you after you get married. Godly counsel is an excellent way to keep a good maintenance on your marriage.

Here are a few questions you can ask yourself (and be honest with yourself):

1. Are you willing to put your spouse before everyone else?

2. Can you be trusted (no secrets)?

3. Can he trust you with the finances?

4. Are you responsible and mature (take care of your business)?

5. Do you watch what you say or say whatever you think?

6. Do you get along with his family and friends?

7. Have you both talked about kids and how you want to raise them?

8. Have you both talked about each other's expected role in this marriage?

9. Have you both talked about sex and the frequency (how often)?

10. Have you both talked about boundaries with the opposite sex?

11. Have you both talked about where you want to live?

12. Have you both talked about your dreams and goals (purpose)?

13. Have you both talked about each other's debt?

14. Have you both talked about how to handle an argument or disagreement?

15. Have you both talked about some outlets and hobbies?

16. Have you both talked about the ability to work through issues (not avoid them)?

17. Have you both talked about what happens when you

don't get your way?

18. Have you both talked about what will happen if issues don't seem to get better?

19. Have you both talked about what patience and commitment look like?

20. Have you both talked about the top three things you need from each other?

Just remember, the issues and problems you currently have will be magnified once you get married. Can you honestly say you can handle it, even if the issues and problems get worse?

I would advise you to talk to your husband every year about question #20, because as you both grow together, your needs may change. Also, I recommend you read *The 5 Love Languages* by Gary Chapman. This book will help you to understand your spouse and he's love language.

CHAPTER 8

Beyond the Third YES!

Being the blessing

Congratulations! The day that you may have been waiting for all your life has arrived. You have implemented the tips and tools that will continue to have a major impact on your marriage. I know a lot of the things mentioned in this book have challenged you and equipped you for the ministry of marriage. I believe that when the storms come (and the trials) that were meant to destroy your marriage, you will be prepared and able to stand on a solid foundation of God's word.

The power of a prayer life

It's important for you and your husband to establish a strong prayer life. Prayer is our best weapon of defense and counter-attack when the challenges come and your marriage gets tested. You will find that the fight and challenges are not a physical fight. It's not even a fight that can be won by arguing. Fighting beyond prayer will cause you to lose every time because you're fighting the wrong enemy. This tactic is at work in a lot of marriages when the husband and/or wife is not spiritually mature. As you mature, you will always be able to see the true enemy. Prayer should always change you first. It is selfish to focus on the faults of others. You must be honest about your contributions to what is not working. Once you're able to discern how to improve yourself, you will be in a better position to be a positive and impactful contributor to your marriage. If you do not view prayer and marriage this way, you will keep the cycle of arguing, bitterness, and disagreements going.

Dealing with your spouse's friendships and affiliations (his family, friends, co-workers)

When you marry him, you also have to accept all that comes with him. This could be challenging at times, because some of the people who are in his life and important to him may not always accept you. Your husband has to set the tone for these relationships. For example, when it came to his female friends, my husband gave them my number, and when they needed certain advice, he encouraged them to ask his wife. If they were real friends, they had no problems being friends with me. They eventually stopped calling him and just called me. In fact, some of the closest people to me now were his friends first. You don't have to feel intimidated by their relationship; simply find a way to connect with her. Make sure your motives are right. Don't just befriend her because you don't trust her, but because you really want to get to know her. If you don't trust her, then your husband may not need to continue being friends with her. Do your best to be friendly and give her a chance to connect with you. Remember, you're an extension of your husband, so if it's important to him, it should be important to you.

Sometimes it's a challenge for the family to accept you. Especially your husband's mother. They want the perfect wife for their perfect boy and these are two words that don't exist, "perfect" and "boy." No one is perfect, and he is no longer a boy. It may seem that you will never be good enough for her son. Family's expectations of you can be unrealistic, and it can drive a wedge between you and them. Don't put your husband in a place where he has to choose between you and his mother. You must find a way to respectfully agree to disagree with her line of thinking and perspective. Just because you don't agree, it doesn't mean you can't find things about her that you like and appreciate and simply focus on that. Give her time (maybe even years) to see your heart and to know that you only want what's best for her son. Out of everyone in his life, his parents may be the most important, and they should be important to you as well. You have to learn how to master these relationships without making things hard on your husband.

Becoming a part of his world

You also have to learn how to fit into your husband's life beyond the home. When you feel like you don't fit in, the first thing you may want to do is to try to pull him away from those people or activities. You may feel intimidated or a little out of your comfort zone. But if it's not life-threatening, you should find a way to enjoy it. He has his life, which includes the things he enjoys, and he just wants you to be a part of it. He wants you to love his friends/affiliations and enjoy some of the same activities. When I first got married, I didn't watch a lot of sports or play video games, and I had no interest in Star Wars and comic books, but I have learned to enjoy them. There were things he liked and things I liked, but ultimately, we had to find what we liked. As you grow with your husband, recognize those activities you both enjoy the most, and do more of that. Never get caught up in what other couples are doing. Don't compare your marriage to someone else; do what works for your marriage.

Enjoy the journey

Now it's time to enjoy the ride. As long as you continue to perfect yourself, you will be just fine. Remember that in this journey, you will need patience. Your marriage is a marathon, not a sprint. In today's world, we want immediate results and don't give our spouses the time to grow and get better in a particular area. Just know that the wait will be worth it! Many marriages die before they can even start growing. Don't destroy your marriage because you don't feel like being patient with your husband. Also remember to be his safe place, where he can tell you *anything* and not be judged by you. You never want him to be afraid to come to you. When he is not afraid to come to you, your marriage will experience a freedom that other marriages could only imagine. There shouldn't be any other person (except God) who he would rather go to with his hurts, temptations, and frustrations. You need to be welcoming and appreciative when he shares his heart with you and no one else. When you know how to pray, nothing should move you. So relax and be cool, because if you don't, he will come to you after he reacts negatively to a situation (a fall or mistake) when he could have told you beforehand, so you could pray that God would intervene. Know that God will help and be with him. All you have to do is pray and trust God. You NEED God in your marriage. Never lose focus of that.

It's also important to do what works in your marriage and stop doing what's not working. Evaluate yourself daily or weekly and recognize the things you're doing that are hurting the relationship and causing division. Learn to be more proactive, and search for solutions to the problems you face. Keep track of what's working, and keep doing it!

As your husband follows God, trust the God in him to lead you into the promises of God. Trust God, even in bad situations, and never lose faith in your marriage. Remember that trouble is not a reason to divorce. Trouble is where the patience and endurance I've been talking about in this book kick in. Continue to review this book as a reminder and a guide. This will be an amazing journey! I'm so happy for you!

PART 2

Relentless

CHAPTER 9

The Enemy's Secret Weapon

I have found over the years that so many women are very unhappy being wives. In many cases, there is no abuse or infidelity. There is really no reason to feel unhappy or unfulfilled, but they do. As young girls, we look forward to our wedding day. We sometimes start dating at a young age, seeking to be in a committed relationship. We put so much energy into relationships and dating to marry that we miss our purpose. We eventually realize that our God-given purpose is where we will find total fulfillment and true happiness.

When I got married, I was so happy and fulfilled. But after the first year, marriage, I had my first son and was a semester from completing my psychology degree. I wanted to be a counselor and eventually get into industrial psychology. I was previously an office manager and was offered a case manager position as soon as I graduated. That position would have given me the experience I needed to further my career. As soon as I graduated, I went back to apply for that position. I was disappointed to find out that the office was closing in the area, and the position was no longer available. So, in pursuit of my dream occupation at that time, I applied everywhere, and no one would hire me. I was even willing to volunteer, but when my baby was four months old, I found out that baby #2 was on the way. With a new baby and one more on the way, we couldn't afford childcare for both children if I volunteered. I was becoming so discouraged. My husband encouraged me to remain home and be a stay-at-home mom. I was okay with the idea because it made sense. But as time went on, I began to lose my dream, identity, and desires for what I imagined my life to be as a mother and wife. My life came to a halt, and it was all about being a stay-at-home mom. Well, I didn't even know what that looked like. My mother worked a 9-5 job, and I'd thought I would too. My mom was also 36 when she had her first and only child, and I was 27 when I had my first child (big difference). I remember my mom being content with her career and not at a place where she was trying to find her purpose.

Since I couldn't work in my desired occupation, I felt like I had to redefine myself. I began to think that maybe that wasn't God's plan for me. So, I sought God for my purpose. During this time, I felt so lost and unfulfilled. I was bad at being a stay-at-home mom because I was unorganized. I stayed on YouTube, trying to get tips on how to be better. It was a life of cooking and cleaning (all day long). I felt trapped in this life that I was not good at. My husband was patient and helpful, but I still became depressed. It seemed like life would always be like this. It's hard to enjoy life doing something you're not good at.

As I continued to seek God, He began to reveal His purpose. Our church began to do women's encounters with God, and I was chosen to be one of the teachers/guides. This was a weekend for women to reconnect with God and be healed and delivered from your past. Since I have a gifting of counsel and teaching, this was total fulfillment for me. I left those weekends drained from the outpouring and ministering that went on, but I loved it and was always ready for the next one. I just loved to see God perform miracles right before my eyes. I knew that this was definitely connected to my purpose in some way.

Another clue to my purpose came a few months before I had my second child. God led me to research and take a course on being a life coach. This also lined up with my gifting, so I studied this business. When I was around seven months pregnant with my second baby, I started a coaching business. I started by doing it for free until I was confident enough to charge. My first few paying clients either wanted to start a new business or were existing business owners. I remember God revealing to me that I needed to focus on business owners and helping them grow their business. I was comfortable as a life coach because I had some life experiences and training. The course I had studied prepared me to work with business owners, but I felt that I didn't have a successful business at the time because I was just getting started. What I didn't know was that it was going to be a long journey to get to where I was meant to be. So after having my second child, I continued to work on building my business. When my two children were one and two, I was pregnant with baby #3. There were times when I stopped seeing clients because I needed to focus more on being a stay-at-home mom. So I studied for years and only worked with one or two clients a year. I was good at my business but couldn't pursue it like I really wanted to. My family was a priority, and I had to do what was best. At times, I felt like giving up on my business. But that was the best time in my life to study and perfect my craft. I watched and helped other businesses grow. I had to remain content. It was such a hard season for me, but a very necessary season. I learned so much and grew professionally during that time. It was a nine-year journey that I refused to quit. Most of all, I see now that my children needed me to pour into them for all those years.

I share all of this to say that when I was single, all I really wanted to be was a wife and mother. I got it and still was unfulfilled. I didn't realize the importance of purpose until I lost what I thought was my purpose. Once you tap into purpose, true fulfillment will come. This is a process that only God can lead you through. I just hate that I had to seek it after marriage. If I could do it all over again, I would have sought God in high school concerning my purpose. But at that time, all I could think about was boys. Just being honest. If purpose would've been pulled out of me at a younger age, I would've been further ahead. Marriage should've been a bonus to the life of purpose that was already created. It's a challenging journey that most women don't have to go through. Still, I have found that there are so many wives just like me who have put their dreams aside to be the mom and wife their families need. We feel very guilty for even wanting to take time away from our families to pursue our dreams. It seems very selfish to want it all.

I have found that those who are in their purpose and then get married are much happier and fulfilled. They have the best of both worlds. They may even stop their purpose to start a family, but their purpose is still there whenever they are ready to go back. They seem content with who they have become. They're at a place where they can just keep adding to their purpose. I believe that God desires for us to be purpose-driven, and marriage is the bonus to your purpose. Many of us women are missing purpose, and then we blame our spouses for them not making us happy. But the truth is that purpose hasn't been pulled out of us, and that is the void.

My husband and I are strategically pulling purpose out of our daughter. I don't want her to go through the challenges I went through. My prayer is that she remains focused on her God-given purpose, so she can be totally fulfilled in life. I encourage you to do the same with your daughters, granddaughters, and nieces. I believe that hidden purpose has been the devil's secret weapon to us never getting to a place where we are totally fulfilled. The devil loves ungodly cycles and generational curses. His goal is to keep us from allowing God to flow through us. But God's purpose is designed to keep us in pursuit until we find it. We feel lost without it. God wants His will here on earth, and He uses us to fulfill His purpose and plans.

It's so important to seek God and His direction for your life. Stay in alignment with the plans God has for you because, in the end, it's all that matters. Alignment positions you to be relentless in your purpose and effective in your marriage. In this next section, we will go deeper into what it's like for a wife to be relentless as a believer.

CHAPTER 10

What Does Relentless Look Like?

In order to be relentless, you have to train your ear to hear God and be willing to obey what you hear. It's time for you to be sure of what God is really saying. Your emotions, the way you feel, is your flesh, and the flesh always leads us astray. It keeps you outside of God's will and in these ungodly cycles. We become entangled in sin and bound, not knowing how we got entangled and not strong enough to break free. But if you stay in a place to clearly hear God and obey, you will experience the fullness of God. No longer will you be confused, deceived, and led astray. If you're ready to be more confident in knowing that you heard from God, keep reading!

We sometimes believe that prayer is all about submitting our request and it being approved. But prayer is so much more than that. It's a two-way communication between you and

God. Once you finish talking, stay still to hear His response. In His response, He may give you ideas, conformation, direction, correction, rebuke, clarity, wisdom, vision, peace, and much more. He also reminds you of His last response if you didn't obey it.

Many times, we look for a new response from God and refuse to obey all previous responses. Since God is all-knowing and knows the end, He is always ready to give you the next step that leads you in the direction you need to go. This is why it's important not to compare yourself or your process to anyone else. You are graced to be who you are, and no one else. Staying in alignment with God's will needs to be what you seek on a daily basis. You can never go wrong in His will. Even when bad things happen, if you're in God's will, He promises to turn it around for your good. "And we know that all things work together for good to them that love God, to them who are the called according to his purpose" (Romans 8:28 KJV). Nothing you go through will be wasted. So, you can trust God to do His part. However, it requires you to not only have faith but to be obedient to your part. Whether you do or don't do, your part affects the outcome.

It seems as if we forget that we have a major part in how everything plays out in our lives. We show God we trust Him through our obedience, especially when He asks us to do something we don't understand or don't want to do. When you live a life of obedience, you will take your salvation to a whole new level. On this level, you see who God really is and how to flow with Him. As you mature in God, you're expected to seek Him for everything. "But seek ye first the kingdom of God, and his righteousness; and all these things shall be added unto you" (Matthew 6:33 KJV). You don't have to seek a word from everyone else (all the time) when you have access to get your own word. There is nothing wrong with *receiving* a word from someone else occasionally, but you shouldn't *seek* it out of others. If they have a word for you, they will share it with you. You have to get to a place where you can trust your ear to hear from God.

Spirit-led life

You will be led by the spirit of truth (the Holy Spirit). Our steps are ordered by the Lord, and we depend on Him to guide us in the right direction for our life (see Psalm 37:23). Honestly, we have no clue as to where to go without the Holy Spirit. The Holy Spirit is a counselor and helper given to us to teach us and remind us of all things (see John 14:26). It's dangerous to be led by our own understanding, because our understanding is so limited. "Trust in the LORD with all thine heart; and lean not unto thine own understanding. In all thy ways acknowledge him, and he shall direct thy paths" (Proverbs 3:5-6 KJV). When we as Christians don't depend on the Holy Spirit, we can live a life of frustration. We question God and become convinced that salvation doesn't work. The truth is we do part of the Bible and expect the full benefits of our salvation. We can't expect the fullness of God without being led by His spirit. It doesn't work that way. As you learn more about God and His character through the Bible, you will learn His voice. The Bible is your guide and will help you to recognize God's voice.

How will you know that God is speaking to you?

» You will be aware of God's presence during prayer, worship, or in an atmosphere where you're tuned in to hear (this could be anywhere).

» Your faith will increase, because what you heard is confirmed in your spirit and lines up with the Bible. It sounds like God and His character.

» You will experience a peace that you may not be able to explain or understand (see Philippians 4:7-9). Always go with the peace that is settled in your spirit. When you have no peace (or feel uneasy) about a situation or decision, you have to acknowledge God (see Proverbs 3:6). Seek God's direction before making a decision. This lets God know you care what He thinks, and you want Him to guide your decisions.

If you want God to speak more often, remain obedient on a consistent basis. The more you obey, the more He will speak. Why would God keep speaking to someone who refuses to listen or obey? "And why call ye me, Lord, Lord, and do not the things which I say?" (Luke 6:46 KJV) Decide daily that you choose to obey God and that your flesh (your will) will not take over. If you struggle with your flesh, ask God to help you overcome this temptation.

What hinders you from hearing God?

- » Too busy (fleshly works)

- » Disobedient (rebellion)

- » Unforgiving (hardened heart)

- » Not sensitive (not aware)

- » The need to repent (live in condonation)

- » Wavering faith (expect to hear)

- » Ungodly thoughts (no peace)

- » Legalism (see Romans 14)

- » Ungrateful (attitude)

- » Half-hearted interest (not pursuing God and His word)

A lifestyle of fasting and praying positions you to hear from God. It will help you to remove all distractions and give your attention to Him. Get a journal and Bible during the times of fasting to write down all God has revealed to you. You need this time to get close and quiet enough to hear from Him. When you know what God is saying to you about the things that concern you, the peace of God will settle your spirit.

When we ask God something, we have no problem receiving the "yes" or permission to get or do what we want. We sometimes get an attitude with God when He says "no" or "wait." God may not say anything at all, and that is still an answer. Don't ignore a response that doesn't give you what you want and when you want it. You have to mature and work on submitting your will to God's will. This will prepare you for those times when your husband will say no or wait. You can't have a tantrum until you get your way. You can't manipulate him to get what you want. You don't get into a relationship with God only to get what you want. If you do that with God, you will do it in your marriage. You will look very immature to your spouse, and that will put your husband in a situation where he doesn't know how to tell you no. He will eventually start to merely tolerate you and begin to become cold toward you. This gets old after a while and could possibly destroy your marriage. God will allow your husband to see things you don't see, so you have to trust the God in him. This is why it's so important that your husband has a relationship with God and can hear God's voice. So, if you submit to God, it will be easier to submit to your husband.

Develop a habit of taking moments to stop and see what you sense in your spirit. Your soul and mind could be overwhelmed with anxiety. Negative thoughts and fear will fill your mind. Take captive those thoughts and cast them out. "Casting down imaginations, and every high thing that exalteth itself against the knowledge of God, and bringing into captivity every thought to the obedience of Christ" (2 Corinthians 10:5). Those thoughts must go so you can clearly hear God. Cry out to God, and He will set you free.

Soul vs. Spirit

Who is speaking, soul or spirit? Your soul tells you what you think, feel, know, and want. Your soul needs to be restored. Your spirit tells you what God thinks, feels, and wants. Your spirit senses God's presence and gives you revelation (a deeper sense of knowing).

All God wants is our obedience. You have two choices: You can be led by God, or you can be led by your flesh. You can't do both and be an effective Christian. Your will gets in the way of God's will. So, will you surrender or rebel?

Ask God, "What do you want me to know?" All you need to do is ask God for wisdom and have faith (see James 1:5-8). If you don't include faith, you will become double-minded and unstable. After the act of obedience, God always gives us the next step. The more you follow these steps, the more peace you will experience – even when things don't seem to be working out for you. That's when the peace of God will come over you, and you can't seem to understand or explain it to anyone. "And the peace of God, which passeth all understanding, shall keep your hearts and minds through Christ Jesus" (Philippians 4:7 KJV). When you know that you have been obedient, you can rest better at night. You may not understand everything that's going on in your life, but you will have peace.

It's important to not be led by your emotions. An emotional decision is a set-up to trap you in a situation you may not know how to get out of. It provides no peace over time. Lack of peace is the indication that something is wrong and you need to go in a different direction. As soon as you begin to experience this, you must stop what you're doing and hear from God. God speaks all the time, but we let our emotions get in the way. Get calm and get rid of all anxiety because God is speaking.

Get alone to seek God. Be still! Put God first, which means work your schedule around God. Daily, ask Him, "What do you want me to do?" Ask Him, "What don't you want me to do?" Go to God first instead of doing what you want, and then turn around and ask God to fix it (see Matthew 6:33). This is not something you only do as a single woman; it continues in your marriage. This is when the relentless side of you shows up. God created marriage, and you have to go back to the source, which means God is the only one who knows how to make your marriage a success. Even after many years of marriage, you will still need God to teach you how to be a better wife. If your focus is to always be the best version of yourself through your obedience to God, you are definitely relentless! So, stay focused! Be ready and relentless because your husband is on the way!

Appendix

Prayers

My prayer for you

I pray that after today, you will never question your worth and never question whether you're enough. I pray that you will heal from every experience that left you broken. I pray that God will help you to forgive and to cut every ungodly soul tie. I pray that you will remove every ungodly desire and appetite. I pray that you are made whole and complete. I pray against every generational curse that is over your life. I pray for the peace of God. I pray for the strength of the Lord to be upon you and that your relationship with Him is the strongest it's ever been. I pray for discernment and the willingness to obey the will of the Lord. I pray that God gives you wisdom far beyond your years.

I pray that you feel the love of God throughout this book and receive His grace that will get you through this season, according to 2 Corinthians 12:9. I pray that God preserves you, and the Holy Spirit keeps you in this season. I pray that you are transformed by the renewing of your mind, according to Romans 12:2. I pray that God maximizes your potential and stirs up every gift that is within you in this season.

Lord, I thank you that in seasons of stretching and more responsibility, it only means that you're making room for the increase and overflow in her life. I ask you to remove spiritual blindness and deafness. I come against the weariness and depression that's on her that is causing spiritual and personal paralysis. I pray that she goes after everything you have for her and doesn't put life on hold while waiting for her spouse. I pray that her obedience to your will, you will give her the desires of her heart. God, cleanse her heart and tear down every wall that prevents her from loving again. Help her to trust you with her life. Help her to overcome every obstacle that she faces. God, strengthen every area where she is weak. Lord, lead and guide every step she takes. Thank you, Lord, for being in total control over everything. We believe and trust that your timing is perfect. So, let your perfect will be in her life. In Jesus' name, I pray. Amen

Prayer of salvation or re-dedication

If you don't know Jesus or have a relationship with Him and want one, start by praying this prayer:

Lord, I want to get to know you and have my own personal relationship with you. I accept you into my heart to be my personal Lord and Savior. I believe in my heart and confess with my mouth that Jesus is Lord. I believe that you died on the cross and rose from the dead. I ask you to forgive me for all of my sins and rebellious ways. I believe by faith that I am saved! In Jesus' name, I pray. Amen.

Congratulations! Next, you will need to find a local ministry where you can learn more about God and grow spiritually. Find someone to mentor you, someone to be accountable to. You're not alone in this walk, and it's helpful to have someone to encourage and guide you as you grow in God. That way, when challenges come, your mentor can help you maneuver through them. Give God the time and opportunity to renew your mind. In this journey, make sure to give yourself time to grow. Never stop pursuing God when challenges come. Challenges are always opportunities for God to increase your faith in Him. God loves you and will always be there for you. Commit to the process. Continue to seek and pray to God on a daily basis, and He will begin to reveal himself to you. I am excited because this is your opportunity to be all that God created you to be, and there is no limit as to how far you can go.

www.ingramcontent.com/pod-product-compliance
Lightning Source LLC
LaVergne TN
LVHW021350080426
835508LV00020B/2209